1 | 95

BLACK HEART

POEMS

BY

GREG FIELD

for Kelly Barth
a bit of humor
and more on the
our pages

MAMMOTH PUBLICATIONS
LAWRENCE, KANSAS

ISBN: 978-1-939301-85-7
LIBRARY OF CONGRESS CONTROL NUMBER: 2014938953

Additional copies may be ordered by mail or email.
Mammoth Publications
1916 Stratford Rd., Lawrence, KS, 66044
www.mammothpublications.net
mammothpubs@gmail.com

Typesetting support from Blue Heron, Silver City, N.M.

DEDICATION:

To Kenneth Field, Viola Field, Jeff Field, and Denece Field. We all started out on this trek together.

To all my grandparents and great grandparents, scattered throughout the Midwest soil, forgive me, your secrets are out.

To Crystal MacLean-Field for believing in my early attempts at writing. To Robert Stewart for helping to hone several of these poems.

To Denise Low-Weso and Tom Pecore Weso for believing this book was worthy of publication.

To Maryfrances Wagner for her understanding, support and editorial expertise in getting many of these poems ready for publication.

INTRODUCTION

When I first heard Greg Field read from this manuscript, I understood that an underground sea of knowledge informs his writing. Dreams, broken lineages, cultural histories, griefs— all add subterranean layers of complexity to his verse. He uses incomplete narratives to fill in lost histories, like the stories of his Potawatomi father, a man whose love appears in paradoxical gestures:

> He said, "Walk quiet in the woods
> like your grandfather's ghost."
> He had two fathers and neither was a ghost.

This "grandfather's ghost," invoked before the death of the actual grandparents, is a spirit that lives within the very real stories beyond margins of these pages.

Other stories haunt this collection. Field's Jewish great-grandmother survived pogroms, only to become an outcast again in the United States. The death of Field's first wife wends through the pages also, a parallel life that occurs on another plane of existence. Field depicts his scenes clearly, yet the broken images he invokes add further powers.

Always, a lyric sense intensifies this poet's lines. Echoes of other media reverberate in his phrasings, as in this painterly scene, excerpted from the title poem "Black Heart":

> I watch the pulsing dot
> of the blackbird as it disappears
> into the dark-blue space
> between the Moon and Venus.
> A punishing shiver vibrates
> my shoulders as I recognize
> the pumping black wings
> are my heart.

Field is a talented man—artist, musician, and poet. All skills appear in the visual, aural, and verbal array of the blackbird as it turns into heart chambers. Such transformation is one of the markers of Field's work, creating dynamic shifts, like the rumbling earthquakes he describes.

The range of poems in *Black Heart* creates a subtext of color, image, rhythm, and melody. Balance of foreground and background, or their imbalance, suggest more tensions. Sometimes Field resolves these with humor, sometimes not. Always, the poems bring to light new understandings.

The most elusive figure in this collection is the narrator. The poet voices experiences from the margins of survival, resetting them centrally in a larger field of vision. Identity is a shifting focal point.

Throughout the book, Greg Field expresses the need for beauty in even the most desperate circumstances. This is an extraordinary collection of painterly poems, one to be read and re-read, one to keep on a table close by. It is a book to hold close to the heart.

Denise Low, 2014

TABLE OF CONTENTS

"An Indian is an Indian regardless of the degree of Indian blood or which little government card they do or do not possess."

— Wilma Mankiller

"In 1890, Indians named 'No Neck' and 'Black Heart' testified in an inquiry before the Office of Indian Affairs. The hearing weighed the morality of Indian employment in show business. 'You are engaged in the exhibition or show business,' observed the acting commissioner, A.C. Belt. 'It is not considered among white people a very helpful or elevating business. I believe that which is not good for the white people is not good for the Indians, and what is bad for the white people is bad for the Indians.'

The Indians defended their work as adamantly as any white performer, and they turned the inquiry into a pointed denunciation of the Indian policy by comparing conditions in the show with those of the Pine Ridge Agency. The contrast reflected poorly on the Office of Indian Affairs. Rocky Bear began by pointing out that he long had served the interests of the federal government by encouraging the development of Indian reservations. He worked in a show that fed him well; 'that is why I am getting so fat,' he said, stroking his cheeks. It was only in returning to the reservation that 'I am getting poor.' If the Great [White] Father wanted him to stop appearing in the show, he would stop. But until then, 'that is the way I get money.' When he showed his inquisitors a purse filled with $300 in gold coins, saying 'I saved this money to buy some clothes for my children,' they were silenced.

Black Heart, too, denounced the allegations of mistreatment. 'We were raised on horseback; that is the way we had to work.' Buffalo Bill Cody and Nate Salsbury 'furnished us the same work we were raised to; that is the reason we want to work for these kind of men.'"

—Louis S. Warren

Song before Going to War

I am going to walk far, far,
I hope to have a fine morning somewhere.
I am going to run far, far,
I hope to have a good night somewhere.

— Traditional

"An old man spoke to his grandson: 'My child," he said, 'Inside everyone there is a battle between two wolves. One is Evil. It is anger, jealousy, greed, inferiority, lies, and ego. The other is Good. It is joy, peace, love, hope, humility, kindness, empathy, and truth.' The boy thought for a moment. Then he asked, 'Which wolf wins?' A moment of silence passed before the old man replied. And then he said, 'The one you feed.'"

— Traditional

THE PERCENTAGES

My father taught me how to track and stalk.
He said, "Walk quiet in the woods
like your grandfather's ghost."
He had two fathers and neither was a ghost.

My grandmother said that each
was the greater of two evils.
She said this with her eyes, not with her words.
She told me one grandfather was pure Potawatomi
and the other was the pure antidote.
She said this on her deathbed.

My father said, "Walk quiet in the woods
like your grandfather's ghost.
You can sneak up on a white man
and slit his throat."
He laughed in the cold duck blind
and pulled two gulps of whiskey.

That night, I looked in the mirror and saw
I was white as the bathroom light.
I followed the smooth line
of my throat where it pulsed
with the words of ghosts.

PASSING

My grandmother and grandfather
Coffeyville, Kansas, 1943

The southeast Kansas winter
and northeast Oklahoma winter
are cold, stillborn twins
laid out in frilly white shrouds.
He crosses over easily
into the town where
the Clantons were shot.
He's an excellent pilot.
He navigates the icy streets
for as long as it takes
to woo the white girl
with the long brunette hair,
to gently lay her down
on the trunk of his Ford.

People hold their tongues
with their mottled teeth.
They let him pass
and winter passes away
 a full nine months.
About the growing belly
they set their tongues loose.
The trip into town
for flour and sugar
spoils the bread.
The wedding poisons the well.
He ships out to fly fighters.

Soon she carries a sister
for her son.
She learns the border
is redrawn, a blood red line
across a farm road.

The pilot returns a hero,
in some other city.
His medals and commendations
never reflect the woman
or the two half-breed kids,
never mention "Potawatomi."
Medals arrive in a box wrapped
in paper the color of their skin.
She gets the news and marries
a sailor far away from the sea.

LEARNING TO DRINK BEER

My father taught me to shoot a rifle.
He said, "A day may come when
the Safeway is closed to you
or the distance to a trading post
is too great. You'll have to hunt
for meat." He drained a bottle
of Pabst Blue Ribbon and walked
down the fence line toward
the empty barn. He jammed
the empty's neck over
a sixty-penny nail he'd pounded
into the top of an old hedge post.
He stood behind me and said,
"Break the bottle."

I jacked a shell into the chamber,
pulled off a shot. The barn wall
ate the bullet. "You'll be one
hungry son-of-a-bitch, boy,"
my father said and slapped
the back of my head.
He drained another Pabst
and sat it at my feet.
I squeezed off another shot.
The fence post shook
and the bottle clanked a warning.

He drained another Pabst,
placed it at my feet,
and slapped the back of my head.
"Who do you think will help you

the day you starve to death.
Your grandmother doesn't
like Indians." I steadied myself,
fired a third shot.
The brown bottle shattered.

"Now go and clean up
all that glass, boy," he said.
I picked up the sharp debris
from tractor ruts. I looked
at a sixty-penny nail bent
like a man's will in the wind.

BLESS THE NERVOUS CHICKENS

I found her letters caught in the pasture fence.
Six years old, I didn't understand abandonment,
or abandon, a woman calling out a man,
the widower Johnston, his, the next farm house
down the county road. I listened to wind
worry paper. It drove me into the center
of the clover field. I lay down in possible
good luck and sun the color of red jello
shown through my hand shielding eyes.
I was lost under the day.

The barn door was left open for years.
A giant black hole in a ramshackle,
red Valentine. From the loft
I saw into the second floor bedroom,
low lamp-light. The approach, their distance,
the silence between coyote calls. Mornings,
I recalled the chickens seemed happy to see
our faces without long noses and tufted ears.
I told Grandfather about the creek littered
with crawdad shells and claws. He said
we were surrounded by hungry thieves.

That evening, I walked out of the clover
after Grandmother opened the kitchen door
and light fanned out through the dark.
I came into the fragrance of fried chicken.
We heard the birds in the coop make a ruckus.
My Grandfather blessed the nervous chickens.
We were all hungry. We were all thieves.

I Am Feeding You, Father

Father, you fell to pieces.
I've collected each chunk
as we go along the trail.
They are bloody bone,
sharp and cut my fingers.
They've worked their way
into my skin. Too deep, so
I dream of all your longings:
women who live in their bodies,
beer that makes my nose run,
whiskey that bleeds the gut.

Tonight I eat sharp cheese
and drink red wine, feeding
those pieces to keep them strong.
On the trail, we are always
on the hunt for more food.
To keep you talking,
I turn and ask you to teach me.
You look at my eyes.
You say, "Take the head shot,
quick kill — eat what you hunt.
If it's not for eating, its spirit
steals a full night's sleep."

LAS VEGAS 21

It is a gift my father insists on.
It is a celebration: a strip club,
a beer I order for myself.
He believes I've never been
in the presence of a naked woman.

It is true. Only my hands have
seen under clothes with kisses.
It is a gift my father insists on—
to fill the space around me
with fragrances and volumes
of legs, hips, backs and bellies,
breasts. The music slaps
the back of my head and
girls enter smiling above
an army of upturned faces.

Their runway parts the sea
of broad shoulders, their legs
up there end in open-toed heels.
My eyes follow the glistening
pubes as a girl thrusts hers against
my big Potawatomi nose. I see
my father's eyes follow each girl's
properly pert and rouged nipples.

A girl works her way down to me,
sways muscled thighs, blue-veined
skin, and passes her breasts across
my face. "Don't look away,"
she whispers. She holds and

caresses me with her eyes.
It is a gift my father insists on,
an embarrassment of riches,
a farewell to the pleasantries
of dreams, this invitation to the dance.

The Truth of Angels

Debra Black stands in the doorway
of the abandoned garage we've broken into
her eyes dark as the water below, lily pads
waiting above their shadows for the sun.

My father calls to the fish in those shadows,
says, "Son, we must be quiet now
or the fish will think we're drinking."
With a rusty church key he deftly opens
a Pabst and releases the stink of every bar
gig I've trailed him through, him carrying
his bass fiddle to the band stand, me darting
in and out of its shadow. He would lift me
onto the bar and shout,

"Give my boy a Shirley Temple —
heavy on the temple!
He knows the names
of fifty god-dammed dinosaurs!
Want to hear'em?"

A couple of the regulars would always turn
to look as if I were a talking dog.
I'd blurt out, "Triceratops, Tyrannosaurus Rex,
Ichthyosaur — a big ancient fish."
Then I would sip my faux drink.

The boat drifts
deeper among the lily pads.
The insects and birds
sound like laughter in the dark garage.

Debra Black whispers,
"Try to find me in the old car."
I find her sitting like an Egyptian statue
in the back seat of the black 'saurian hulk.
A bit of sunlight from a broken window
illuminates her light blue tee shirt.

"Wake up boy! The fish are moving.
They're insulted—your rod tip
in the water, your chin in your chest!"

I remember a morning boating back home.
Up in the blue sky, a remnant of the moon
disappears behind circling seagulls.

Wings flash white against the light blue. I try
to breathe when the wind crosses the bow
taking my breath away.

My Jewish Experience

I sit with my mother
sipping water. She's decided
to tell her grandmother's story.
A young Jew escaped a pogrom,
escaped Lithuania, sailed
to America. She took up
with a well-to-do doctor.

He installed her as his mistress
in a fine apartment
in downtown Kansas City.
Six years later, he stuffed her
clothes into a valise, threw it
out a window, and hustled her
and her two bastards out
to the street. Bid her good day
and walked away.

I never told my mother
about the box I found
while exploring the attic
at seven. I lifted
the grey lid with a dim
flashlight and revealed
the impossibly tall piles
of bodies behind barbed
wire. Eyes in skin-wrapped
skulls stared into my eyes.

She brings out the box
of photographs and explains
how her USO unit followed
the troops so closely
they often arrived only hours
after the Germans had fled.

Years ago, I'd wondered
how all those people
had gotten so thin. Being
asthmatic, I'd feared
for their breathing the way
they were piled up
like old pillows. Now
I knew they were all dead.

I said this to her. "No,
she said, "they weren't
all dead." Some GIs noticed
several atop the pile
still breathed. They pulled
them down, gave them water
and food. It killed them
within a few minutes. She
said the GIs were stunned
and some cursed and cried.
They thought they'd
saved those spirits.

REFUGEES

Like two refugees on the road from Ypes,
he holds her hand as they limp along.
She is full-faced into March wind. Her hair
flies out with each gust. Her jaw clenched,
her face scarred red, she leans into him
and they roll. As if on a bent hinge,
his leg swings out sideways. Like a tank,
a bus roars by spewing dark, poisonous gas.
They emerge, march for a muddy parking lot.

Then I see the red lights of the police cruiser
flash by. The car pulls in at them,
cuts them off. Face to face, the two refugees
gaze at each other as the cruiser's door
springs open like a trap and a pistol is leveled
at them. As they kneel in the mud hands
rising above their heads, shoes tumble
from their jackets like stolen secrets.

I Dream While My Brother Watches for the Sheriff
Frisco, Colorado, 1974

The little red-headed boy
moves toward the john
at the back of the bus.
He walks like a box
with crushed corners.
I nudge my brother,
say, "Look at this guy,
he really knows
where he's going."

In the dream the boy
tilts by, but my brother
shakes me awake
into a summer afternoon
in a strange town square.

A sheriff looks down
where we sprawl
in park grass, the litter
of ham sandwiches and beer.
"You boys know where
you're going?" he asks.
I'm about to say, "Back
to sleep." But my brother,
gathering the garbage,
barks, "Out of town."

How I Fell and Cut My Knees

"I am lost. I'm not sure why." Anonymous

At an early age, I removed my own wings —
used a sharp stone found at the creek's edge,
feathers spun away on the green water.
The pain was anger enough to throw the stone
at a girl passing above on the bank.
She collected my wings, held them out to me
like she later pursed her lips
and presented them for a kiss.
She was miraculous — the dismembered wings
pulsed forward, carried away another rock
from my hand as they spun up into the sky.
My eyes opened wide and I fell
striking my knees on stones in the mud.
My cheeks coursed with tears, came to rest
against her thighs. The mud was red
where my knees struck,
the water cold, the creek real.

THE STORY I TELL YOU

I want to read something to you, because
I love you. Through the window I see
the roofs and cooling units and the useless
chimneys clogged with dead birds.
But I want to read something to you, because
I love you. So I read you the window's story.

I read you the story I see across the glass
and tar paper roofs. The story of the old man
opening the pigeon coop, reaching in slowly
and bringing out a delicate bird
with strong markings, cradled like a heart
just removed from a young, impetuous donor,
and releasing it into the ever expanding sky.

RED BIRDS RISING

We were warned.
As foretold, a cloud
of dark red birds rose
from among the black lumps
of cattle in the steaming fields,
spread and blossomed, became
heaven's bloody morning.

A woman saw them rising,
gathered sleep to her bed.
It cascaded down the dark
red hole of her throat,
boiled and grew in the heat
of her belly that ruptured.
Objects shiny and sharp
flew into the undressed world.

A man gathered wounds
to him, red bandages
draped his white flesh,
his white bones.
This man gathered pain
to him and sang his song
through clenched teeth.
His song is old and slow.

He gathered his breath
and it became a red bird
at his window,
its breast opened
into heaven's morning.

We were warned
of dark red birds
rising. We were warned
about heaven's morning,
and the danger of sleep.

ELEMENTS OF FAITH

Under a moonless sky,
the road up the mountain
was a dark tunnel of pines.
No homesteader's cabin lights.
Anchorage streetlights thirty miles
back, below the sea of night.

The gravel-and-mud washboard
made the old Buick bounce
and squeal. Each creek we crossed
boiled and hissed on the exhaust.
Bill got his shoes wet when icy
water shot in under the rattling door.

He cursed the sudden decision to sleep
on the mountain after a day
skipping classes and an evening
drinking our way from Anchorage
to Bird Creek. Dan kept shouting,
"Moose Pass or bust!" But here
we were climbing an abandoned
access road, headlight blind, peering
past muddy windows for a turn off,
a place to roll out sleeping bags.

When all were silent, eyes rolled
back, the '55 Super's frame
high-centered on a decaying stump.
I climbed out. Sleeping bag bunched
in my arms, a consuming dark cloud,
I stumbled toward a tree's

pine needle pallet, but fell.
On my back, staring straight up
at the uncountable stars I screamed,
Swallow me, now!" "Swallow me up!"
The black maw of the universe licked
my forehead and opened wide.

HOW A BIRD IS BORN

The small one,
the one we carried to the tree,
the one we carried to the river,
the one we carried to the mountain,
and then up through the clatter of rocks,
up past the caves' moaning holes,
up to the tiny table of the peak,
and then to the moist sky.

The sky that draped
our shoulders in shawls of mist,
the sky that granted
only enough air to dance
under the cold sun.
We offered it up
to the darkness
that crouches at the edge
of the blue wind.

The small one,
the one joined with the sky,
the one we carried,
the one we sang
into the blue, into the black,
the black that feeds the stars
and grants the wings
made from all the light.

THIS SEASON OF EGGS

The morning sky after last night's storm
the color of the eggs I find down the block
beneath a peeling birch. The quiet air will
not be disturbed by the tiny, damp feathers
revealed. Another house down I see
a dead fledgling in the grass, pieces of egg
not far from it. It fought its way out
into hell, falling farther than any harlot's
son. Near the cul de sac, a nest of broken
eggs, small birds stumbling about
through weeds, their parents keening
in the limbs above, waiting patiently
with food, refusing to give in, to fly away.

After walking the dogs, I drive to work
among fallen branches, streets awash
in the tides of giant puddles, surfaces
crazed with oil rainbows. Walking
to the door of the research building
I find laid out on the steaming concrete
a fledgling's body blue and naked, eggs
cracked, leaking, strewn in the lawn.
A nest upended, fallen from a niche
at the roofline. This little one was the first
to breath and the last to breath.
The night's visit from world's end
turned the young out into the storm
without a door to make a mark on.

From the Lobby of the Longbeach Hotel

Small birds, yellow and black
strokes of paint, flash among
the palms. A breeze gusts
and whips a fountain's spray
into faces of complaining gulls.
The spars of sailboats ghost
along in the distance, stark
against the Queen Mary's
black hull, preserved on rocks.
Now she shelters all these
elegant sloops returning to
their slips and cleated lines.

In the hotel's lobby
a small black-haired girl
wants adamantly to enter
the revolving door.
She is aware, but her mother
has forgotten, the four worlds
spinning by, how walking
that circle you pass through
each without entering the other
three glass chambers as though
through an unselfish heart,
while keeping in sight
the people outside.
I think if the world weren't
so full of beauty
I wouldn't care to leave it.

129 BLACKBIRDS

My arm is the branch
where the snake uncoiled,
dropped his head and sang in a whisper
only the blackbirds could hear.

One hundred twenty-nine blackbirds
are the leaves of the tree — all
squawking secrets in the snake's song,
secrets as sweet as the song of Solomon.

My tangled hair is barren twigs
left below when their black veil
lifts into the evening air,
a rotating cloud. My body is the tree.

Blackbirds speak in pointed tongues
news in the snake's song — stories of winter
and spring, of desire and kisses,
kisses that will well up the roots,
well up branches and twigs, open
mouths below the sky.

DUCK

We all recognized the crosshairs
behind the colors,
breathed in tiny jerks
behind the golden rushes.

But we landed in liquid sky
among brothers struck dumb,
held our heads up in the breeze,
muttering and duck blind.

THIS CONTRACT

Because I couldn't stop the universe
from killing you, I'm sad, ashamed.
It's hard to compete with something
as large as a billion galaxies.
Once you enter its darkness, it surrounds
you. It touches all of you. You breathe it.

I mill my arms through air, trying
to break the very bonds of molecules,
of atoms. I know nothing of those
sticks and balls, the forces that glue
them together.
              We entered this contract
with the ineffable. Maybe we knew it.
It might have lurked on mountain trails,
or hid behind the doors of temples.
I spoke to a lawyer about suing.
We sipped gin as he bragged
about his billable hours.

I have no recourse to recover my loss.
I have only your name, a picture
of your face. Because I couldn't stop
the universe from killing you,
I'm ashamed.
Broke.
The lawyer advises me
I can never retire.

FALLING ASLEEP ALONE IN DECEMBER

Exposed in a plain of white snow
a dark spot on a white highway,
the motorcar disappears, reappears
within the drift's stout shoulders.

A cold wind brings the strange
ratcheting of an old projector
against the car's rimed windows.

The frames tumble into numbness
that seeps into the motor's heart.
It rattles and quits each night —
the necessary coasting into sleep.

BLACK HEART

Both hover like ghosts
in the morning sky
above the sunlit overpass,
the star and the Moon—
white orb that teaches
the goddess of love
her cycles. As I emerge
from the concrete's
shadow, I see a blackbird
launch itself straight up
at the fading apparitions.

Wind slips through car windows,
feeling like cool fingertips.
I watch the pulsing dot
of the blackbird as it disappears
into the dark-blue space
between the Moon and Venus.
A punishing shiver vibrates
my shoulders as I recognize
the pumping black wings
are my heart.

SALVAGE

After the Good Friday Earthquake Anchorage, 1964

Imagine the tornado,
the flying monkeys.
You have to imagine,
it's too damned cold
here for monkeys,
wings or not. The truth
of a house that flies
over a bluff and lands
in chalky clay belies
the truth of no evil
witch crushed beneath.
Maybe you're the victim,
on your back under there
looking up at broken
braces, copper pipes
like orderly snakes
writhing beneath joists.

No matter. You must
put your hacksaw to work
as your brother creaks
about the jumble teetering
in rooms above. How
unsettling to feel the whole
house shift, a joist pinning
your shins. You calculate
what a whole house weighs
as it shifts again, pressure
rises from your bones.

You're not lying drugged
in a poppy field. So back
to sawing, shiny slice
after shiny slice. It's not
Dorothy, but your sister
at the corner of the house
asking that the salvage
be passed out from inside
the wood and clay coffin.

You hear the pieces
of copper pipe slam
into the red wagon's bed.
The Earth has swallowed
the neighborhood, and you
have become the lucky
entrepreneurs and wizards.

AN EARTHQUAKE DREAM
Anchorage, Alaska, 1964

A steaming crack opens at my feet
as the rumbling and jerking stop
to fade into the sky like thunder.

I collect pebbles and drop them in,
listen to them bounce against the sides—
sharp clicks drop out of earshot.

I imagine a young couple deep below
waiting in the night, snow falling
over their bodies. They are warm
beneath their coats and don't hear
the pebbles fall with the flakes.

What they hear are their lips
meeting. A language of breath
and mist. The drifts of snow muffle
the plunk of the pebbles.
A bus emerges from swirling flakes,
and the two are gone.

IS THIS WHAT YOU MEANT?

What you meant
to the world
arrives in envelopes.
What you did
in the world
is still healing.
As for me,
the stitches will
come out soon.
I have paged through
the cancelled insurance
forms and yellowed music,
read the letter
to your mother about
getting what you hoped
for all the bookings,
expenses, meals, down
the street from the old
hotel, but all the boxes
are not quite full—
a small empty space
remains. I keep on
looking and gingerly
picking over. And there
is the box wrapped
in black paper. It sits
outside the front door.
Now I use the back door
only. Is this what you meant?

THE OLD FRIENDS

All five lying dead in the barn, each to a stall.
She shot her horses and within a week
the whole town knew. The sheriff drove out —
asked her about it. Any strange persons or
cars she'd seen? The loss of these
beautiful animals broke his heart. He wanted
this perpetrator. "I had a rifle," she said
"and I couldn't imagine a reason for them
to be there anymore." He said, "You're very
hurt by this — I can see that. We'll talk
later," he said, "Later." For some time
no one believed her. She had loved
those five horses. The sheriff spent days
and nights searching for the killer.

The shooting of defenseless animals
made him put away his dark glasses
and cowboy hat and then he saw
everything without those shadows and shades.
After about a week, she drove into town
and parked her old GMC in front
of Leon's Hardware, and was followed in
by Ben and Nancy Loy. From behind a rack
of nails and screws, they watched her buy
a black .38 pistol and ask for one bullet.
Ben Loy quietly side-stepped his way out.
He was calling the sheriff when the patrol car
pulled in beside the old GMC. He'd tracked
her since going by her place earlier and seen
her barn burning. He stepped inside Leon's.
At the counter, he gently removed the pistol

from her hands, stuffed it in his belt
at the small of his back. Outside, they sat
in the patrol car. She was surprised to see,
for the first time in years, the sheriff's
full face, his blue eyes, his large forehead
with its receding hairline and creases
like vicious knife slits. "Sam," she said,
"I've lately been suffering from a
terrible lack of imagination."

LETTERS FOUND

I
Looking up through winter branches
I see all the letters you did
or did not write explode from the sky
in a blizzard of cold, melancholy bits.
As if usurped by digital ones and zeroes,
they tumble, a million yeses
and no's, all tiny, torn, and sharp.

II
Before I met you I remember
waking in the median of a freeway
outside San Francisco,
sleeping bag hidden within shrubs.
Not the sound of a single vehicle
to worry my dreams, or block my exit.
I gathered my kit and climbed
up onto an elevated crosswalk.

I heard the approach of a host
of locomotives, rolling of wreck
and ruin going eighty-five.
I saw the wave's multi-colored head
broach a hill and charge
six lanes wide and full until it passed
beneath me like hell's risen army.

III
I heard that sound again
the night the surgeon walked
into the room and sat beside me.

52

I could barely understand
the choices he offered over
the roar of the wave that shook
the walls and chairs. My heart
ceased being muscle. I left you
there where the world ended.

I descended into the concrete
parking structure and listened
to the fluorescent ballasts hum.
I took a breath and felt my blood.

IV
In December, holidays open time
like a peeling cigar box
of this and that—
you pull it down
to do the promised perusal
of concert tickets and old envelopes.
A picture generates a ferocious sound
and you stand in the flakes of letters.

HOLDING MY BREATH

Once I held my breath
under water for a year.
I looked up and concentrated
on the sun, its distorted disk
rippled on the water's surface.

I thought about the time
I was eight and dived
off our dock and held my breath
long enough to pull myself
below its fat fifty gallon barrels.
Within the dock's hollow center,
I surfaced in shafts of sunlight
chopped by the lapping green water.

Over that year I watched months
sink heavy by my shoulders
followed by my love's blouse
and dresses waving by as they settled.

Next, black metal hangers like hooks,
baitless, cartwheeled down; passed
in front of my nose, bubbles drifted
from my nostrils, silver balloons of waste.

I looked up and saw them coming:
earrings, necklaces, bracelets, treasures
sinking through the liquid light.

Finally, the delicate translucence —
her ghost tumbled by, bubbles roiling

about its edges. I almost drew
a deep green breath, but my burned lungs
held as I settled deeper. I followed
the treasures of that life into darker water,
and cold mud where I dreamed—

treading water under our dock's planking
sucking in air, I became aware of the rust
eating away the barrels' flaking sides
and I saw that really, nothing floats.

Graveyard Shift, McCarren Airport

In a men's room stall I do not
disturb the drunk collapsed
between the toilet and the wall,
just swab the floor. It's four
in the morning, I let him sleep.

Outside the sun opens the sky,
blinds the blue eye of heaven.
Another graveyard shift done,
I watch a mirage of water float
over fences and parking lots
as jet exhaust ripples chilly air.

My motorcycle rolls out
into empty streets behind
fountains and lucky casinos.
The ride home's reward —
a roadrunner's rush
after the business of life.

Finally, I sit at the four-way stop,
a mile from home and minutes
from sleep. Immersed in exhaustion
I see a young woman at the wheel
of a Chevy, glide to a stop before
the sign opposite. Her arm rests
along the window, long dark hair
flows across it.
Far up the road something roars,
but I hear her radio sing as her car
rolls into the intersection

and instantly an old Buick appears,
slams into her driver's door.
Her white forehead flashes across
the windshield, her arm flails.

Both vehicles spin away
like lost planets as glass dances
across the asphalt. I am waiting
to begin my crossing, the space
now empty. But I still hear her
radio and I try to identify the song.

THE FOUND CHILD

I am the found child.
The implications are grand
as beautiful eyes seeing
the end of an estrangement,
the capitulation of years
before the mast ending
a life contemplating
my open palm's map.
Searchers range about
crying out my name.
Handbills posted, my picture
oddly shifts like a star
speeding away
into outer dark.

Now rescued and returned
to my parent's house,
I find the insufferable
searchers lounge about
our rooms like old cats.
Sit and rest they inveigle.
I hide on a cramped couch,
breath like an old man
stuttering into tears,
watch my parents hug
and kiss, me forgotten.

DIMMSDALE IN HEAVEN

Before this, what was I?
Could any soul be
closer to God, in his hands
coldly cradled? Might my
pure heart bleed through
to the world if sullied
an iota, pushed a pinch
by some ungracious demon,
some poor evil in the air?
But after all, I was like
other men, neither good
nor evil — just want was
my own worst enemy.
My own cross, then,
was heavier; the builders'
nails sharper. As rigid
as a scaffold, I was wrong.
I thought I was the only
flower to fail, but instead
of bleeding through my own
breast, bled through hers.
Ignorance supped at it
like dandy-dressed flies
and so flew the law.
So, to the physician — No!
To the sea — No!
But yes, to the small arms
of judgment I built, so yes —
a scaffold became
my sweet last cradle.

HELL IN A HANDBASKET

The sky is the color that inspired many sailors
to take warning. I bump into the Devil outside Costco
He hands me a warm handbasket, winks.

"I'm hardly the man for this job, "
I complain. "Don't make my people
call your people," he says and settles
into a black limo. "Go, Moose!" and he's gone.

I never knew the back-story to the expression,
but now we're all going like so many bad eggs.

The Carpacio Family ain't got nothin'
on the horned one. So much for making lunch from
the taste stations, but the aisles are full,
the basket already feels heavy.

THERE'S SOMETHING GOING ON

There's something going on
with my neck. But who am I
to tell? Everyone wants flowers
or money. I could seek out
an adjustment — someone with
big hands, someone with
strong arms to carry
lots of flowers. I gave all
my money to an idea,
an idea that sought
an adjustment. Now I can
visit my dogs only
on Sunday mornings. I must
call ahead, ideas have plans.

There's something going on
with my neck. Someone pointed
out that my head rides on it
at a jaunty angle. Maybe
the angle is what's wrong
with my neck. I know it's
affecting my head. Someone
points me out on the sidewalk
as I walk with my head
at a jaunty angle, my skinny
arms carry so many flowers
no one can see my face.
I can't see where I'm going.
There's something going on.

Radioactive

I received a call from my doctor.
He asked me to his office
as soon as I could get away.
I sat before what had been
a vast redwood forest but was
now the shiny plain of his desk.
His face loomed above it all
like a rare mythic being.
He spoke, "I'm going to put this
right out there — no maple coating.
I'm sad to report
that you're radioactive."
I asked if I was a sender or receiver.
"Both," he said, "and after
further tests, probably a tower, too."

He arose and eventually
made his way behind my chair
from where he placed,
with sad ceremony,
a large red strobe atop my head.
"For your safety and air traffic
safety, too," he said.
I felt the first tingling
of a speed metal tune
like electricity across my teeth.
He patted my shoulders,
"You have three, maybe four
days left. Watch your head."

YOUNG WOMEN MAKE ME SLEEPY

The young women,
their stretched bodies
standing around, butts
jacked up above stiletto heels,
make me sleepy.
In their jeans jackets
they are like
an arrangement of blue
'ludes on a shag rug.

Some friends and I
are about to swallow
a couple each and lie down
with a glass of red wine,
listen to Miles Davis boil
a cauldron of bitches' brew —

until someone mumbles
is that a horn or was it
the young women sighing
into their boyfriends' collars
their hands gathering wads
of material along their
boyfriends' pant legs
like morning bedclothes.

Now I'm back in the moment
I can't keep my eyes open —
all the young women
make me sleepy.

THE WATERWORKS MASTER

You are like the buckeye
my young friend gave me
saying, *Hold on to it,*
it will bring you luck.
I've carried you
like a lump of cinnabar
with a living tube
strung through it--
led out between my thighs.
You've been neutral,
not lucky, until now.
You grow cranky.
You hold your breath and swell.

It's been over half a century,
my dangerous little friend.
What can we say to each other
as we circle like angry dogs?
You started out so small,
so quiet and me so unaware.

Now, you whisper your demands,
tapping me, from inside,
you bloody little valve.
Remember, as you squeeze
that important pipe,
it is such small things
that carry us both toward dark.

EVENING LIKE A STOLEN KISS

A couple comes out of doors, stands
on the porch's edge. Dim light lingers
on red leaves. A breeze looses
their crisp clatter. The air caresses
the tiny hairs on the couple's faces.

Their lips ache in the growing cold.
Touched by the chill their shoulders
shake. Darkness settles in their eyes.
Together they tumble into the Fall —
cast out, blind and in love
with each other's surfaces.

There Is a Spider in the Corner

Light illumines a web above the door.
Ceiling cracks and stains provide
maps for her multitude of eyes
to follow. She is everywhere
at once and in the high corner
from where she sees many ways
to wander, but she squats and stays.

JELLYFISH

Drifting in currents
these hearts pump,
translucent as lingerie.
Full lacy cups, their
filaments of love or desire,
fly like the heart's
many arms. They hide
the sting of a lover's eyes,
a lover's tongue, hot
fingers prying life from
water. They are pretty,
so simple, functional
as kisses, contractions,
or the way women's hips
cradle all creation.

A DARK RIVER

Smooth cold slide of a silver
blade across tight skin —
the crazy white balloon
of the moon pricked by a star
slips deflated to light pole
to asphalt — dirty circle of light.

A dog walking a man stops
sits on his tail in the circle
while the man fashions a prayer
to the moon-empty sky
and dim, sharp stars fall
on the man's naked forehead.

The dog smells the deer hidden
in the dark where they orbit
dew-stained grass, chill earth
the man beckons his hunger
and theirs as it strides
toward the circle of light.

Their hunger approaches
along the path that ends
by a river circling the Earth
as it tumbles through night
evil particles vibrating with music
like a heart attacked by love.

HEAVEN'S DOG

Empty streets are wet with thunder,
with drops of another philosophy.
A ragged dog on the corner is finally empty.
He has given up dreams of meat and milk.

Behind him the chapel's doors are locked.
His acute eyes can see the naked spirits
blinking through the broken glass.
Clouds and sun work together to bathe
the barren chapel's steps in golden light.

A sparrow lands in this nimbus,
boldly snatches an insect from under
the dog's stark belly and hops
into the shadow beneath heaven's dog.

CITY OF DREAMS

Cars each contain a consciousness.
They pass beneath green squares.
Later, they move among orange cones
warning of big holes hungry for
water, scraps, mud and children.
The cars move through the silence
before the first bird feels the heat
of arriving daylight. A car stops
for a woman sucking a brown filter,
sharing her marked breath
with her child in tow. They've seen
the boarded houses, their boards
slathered in graffiti signing
someone's apocalyptic dream.

The cars move by children attending
the school of the front stoop, heads
lolling into the dreams of orange
cones and big holes hungry.
Cars move by people walking
sidewalks, people still immersed
in dreams of bigger guns all
oiled and shiny, people hearing
banter of skulls in the alleys
and backyards smelling of murder.
The cars move through this
beginning, this moment before
the first wave of packed vehicles
seeks its own level in concrete
sluices and conquers the air.

WINTER VISITS

Sweet smoke
and fire create
a dichotomy—
warm cheeks seduced—

flush, but the backs
of necks know
it's like a kiss, cool,
on the forehead.
A shawl is craved.

Cold air, a caul,
surrounds all —
the stars come home,
universe in the backyard.
A chaos of shivers
stalk the cold rooms.

Eyes glance behind.
A visible curse trails.
Magnetic life elsewhere
drags souls away —
cannot linger, but tumble
through the cold air alone.

DREAM, A DREAM

I
You are a nattily dressed lobbyist
for a maker of fine biologics
looking down through
the 80th floor window watching

your mother sink below the stones
of her hospital bed until she slips
below the surface of the asphalt
stream floating the massive city.

II
An old man sits on a wood bench.
He slices open a fresh fig broken
from the crotch of a hand-leafed tree.

He shifts his buttocks and breaks wind.
The cabin's walls grow into trees
and you are a fox by a stream of stones.

II
You are a mantis in a garden.
You pull another insect apart.
You see, but don't understand
the girl lounging on the white chaise.
She picks her nose, till it bleeds.

Her hair is skinny banners caught
in wind that builds till it lifts
beach house's roof shingles.

Rain falls and runs along exposed
trusses and joists and drips through
a spider web's sparkling sieve.
A brown stain bleeds across
the unsullied white ceiling.

IV
The sun sets beyond the highway's edge.
Headlight beams become liquid streams
in a forest where trees grip the ground
while a crowd of charlatans raise a banner
that masks the moon. In the darkness
resulting, you can't find your way
You stumble into trees until you see
light slice the air as a door swings open.

Once inside, you spy an old man
slit open a fresh fig to rich red pulp.
He shifts his buttocks and breaks wind.
You understand the sweetness,
the illumination. You are smiling.
You feel like you've found all the toys
you've lost since you were five years old.
But a fellow sitting way back in shadows
whistles a different dream and that music
turns out the light.

The Dig

Caught in an assistant's sieve
as dust among bone
and painted clay all together.

The same is inhaled
with metal and stone
we grind.

      Thousands
of tiny cilia excavate
and pass up in mucus
swallowed or spit.

It is us
and us all over again.

A Cloud Admonishes Us

The day you spurn him
there is a cloud as dark
as the heart of an apple.

It descends and touches
earth like two fingers to
pinch and pull its surface.

Rain fills all of space,
falls, a multitude of hands
to push down shoulders;
the wet weight of sleep.

The cloud hums a lullaby
as it comes until it's close
and then it howls. It is
night rotating, screaming.

It is the one and only
parent and growls — go
to sleep, quiet down now,
or go to hell and fly.

SOMEONE AND HIS CONTRAPTION

The door is closed.
The door is closed.
No dash of light glows
at its bottom leaking
into the evening dark.

It is inky black
on the other side.

Someone
and his contraption
removed the light
from the other side.

I can go out with you.
We can ask all we meet,
Who was it?
What type of contraption?
Who presented that engine —
sucked away the light?

The door is closed, you say.
I say the door is locked tight,
like a ten thousand dollar
coffin. You've advised me —
No, the door is closed.
The door is closed.

A MORNING WALK

Fog settles on the slick grass.
The morning walk is warm
and Emily, my dog, swings
her tail and like a woman
entering a bar, she walks
as if ignoring all the eyes,
tongues, glass mugs
refracting the low, yellow light.

Emily stops to sniff the small
bumpy Buddhas hopping away.
The street glistens under
a blue-black sky shaded
like my love's eyes before sun
sparks and fills them with light.

CLARITY'S ARROW

Sometimes I must have the world
very close to me. It's not so much
about touch as it is about clarity.
Sometimes the air is thick
as bullet-proof glass and the grass
leaps up at me in a green blur.
I must stop and crouch, observe
each blade so a faint nausea
clears away like a child's memory
of letting fly an arrow straight up
at the sky in an orchard ripe
with rotting apples and crouching
to observe the leather-colored skins,
ruddy and wrinkled, the liquefied
organs leaking into the grass
as the arrow falls, a pointed letter
telling me of my position,
the pink innocence of my scalp
hidden uselessly
by each blade of hair.

THE CURE

I walk on the wave-tumbled stones
of Lake Superior's north shore. Each wave
gathers up the smallest and tumbles them
in froth — red diamonds in white lace.

I carry the wind in my chest, the spray
in my shoes and in my jaw some pain.
We might sit on these smooth stones

and track the origin of the ache as it whines
through my teeth and bone — the sanguine
annoyance of a determined mosquito.

Amid multitudes of stones I spy one
palm-sized, flat and warm with the sun.
Picking it up, I press it against my face.

Its smooth heat soaks into tissue and bone.
My mouth opens into a smile to bless
the luminous lake and its stones.

These poems, sometimes in different versions, previously were published in the following media: "How a Bird Is Born," *New Letters*; "Some One and His Contraption" and "We Entered This Contract," *Thorny Locust*; "Hell in a Handbasket," *To the Stars Through Difficulties* (editor Caryn Mirriam-Goldberg, Mammoth Press); "I Dream While My Brother Watches for the Sheriff," fine edition publication No. 1179 in the Poems-For-All series, San Diego (editor Richard Hansen); "Black Heart" in the River Cow Orchestra album *This Is Not a Bill*.

No Neck and Black Heart quotations come from Louis S. Warren, *Buffalo Bill's America: William Cody and the Wild West Show*, (2005), page 372.

Greg Field is an artist, writer, drummer, sailor, chemist, computer geek, and network administrator. His poems appear in many journals and anthologies, including *New Letters, Laurel Review, Karamu, Chouteau Review,* and *Kansas City Outloud II*. His book of poems *The Longest Breath* (Mid-America Press) was a Thorpe Menn Finalist, and his chapbook *End of This Set* is from BkMk. Field has degrees in painting from the Kansas City Art Institute and the University of Missouri-Kansas City. He was an elementary art teacher for thirteen years. His paintings are in private collections all over the country. He plays percussion in River Cow Orchestra, an improvisational jazz band. Upon his wife's death in 1987, he, Robert Stewart, Miles Sandler and Maryfrances Wagner set up the Crystal Field Scholarship for a student at UMKC majoring in creative writing. Proceeds from the annual Crystal Field Scholarship Reading contribute to that fund.

Black Heart is set in 11 point Californian FB, an American font designed by Frederic W. Goudy (1865-1947). Goudy designed the original font for the University of California Press in 1938. Lanston Monotype Co. released a version in 1956. Digitized additions from 1988 to 1999 are designed by Carol Twombly, David Berlow, Jane Patterson, Richard Lipton, and Jill Pichotta.

* Indicates an E-Book format

Barry Barnes, *We Sleep in a Burning House*, poems, $10

Xánath Caraza, *Conjuro* (English, Spanish, Nahuatl), poems, $18

Robert Day, *Talk to Strangers*, essays from The Land Institute, $8
    We Should Have Come by Water, arts ed. poems, $20
        We Should Have Come by Water, chapbook, $10

Greg Field, *Black Heart*, poems, $15

Diane Glancy, **Now It Is Snowing inside a Psalm*, prose, $12
        Stories of the Driven World, prose, $14
        It Was Then: Diagram of the Elemental, poems, $12

Caryn Mirriam-Goldberg, *Landed*, poems, $12

Caryn Mirriam-Goldberg, editor. *To the Stars: A Kansas Renga*, $18,
    Kansas Notable Book,

Jonathan Holden, *Glamour, poems, $12

Denise Low, editor, *To the Stars: Kansas Poets*, Ks Notable Book, $12

Stephen Meats, *Dark Dove Descending: Poems and Stories*, $12
        Looking for the Pale Eagle, poems, $12

Theresa Milk, **Haskell Institute: 19th Century Stories of Survival*, $20

Lana Wirt Myers, *Prairie Rhythm: Life and Poetry of May Williams Ward*, $14,
    Ks. Notable Book

Caleb Puckett, *Fate Lines / Desire Lines*, poems and prose, $15

Elizabeth Schultz, **White-Sand Dream: Hoopa Stories*, $12

William Sheldon, *Rain Come Riding: Poems*, $12

Pamela Tambornino, **Maggie's Story: Teachings of a Cherokee Healer*, $14,
    hardcover, $24

E. Donald Two-Rivers, *Fat Cats, Powwows: Poems*, 2nd ed., $12

Thomas Pecore Weso, **Wisconsin Indigenous News 1865-1930*, $6

Thomas Weso & Denise Low, *Langston Hughes in Lawrence*, $12

EMAIL ORDER mammothpubs@gmail.com (PayPal)
MAIL ORDER: 1916 Stratford Rd. Lawrence, KS 66044
Add 7% Kansas sales tax, $3 shipping
www.mammothpublications.net